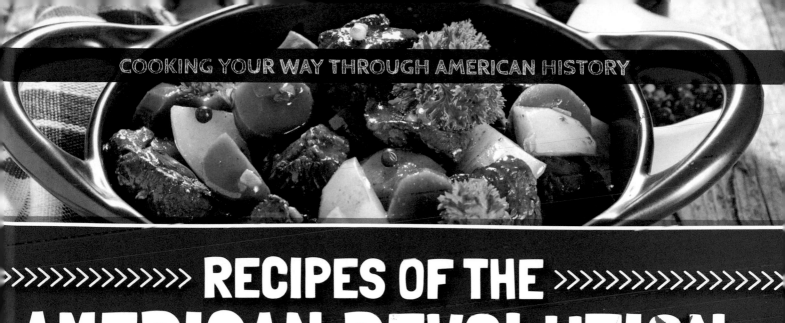

COOKING YOUR WAY THROUGH AMERICAN HISTORY

⫸⫸⫸ RECIPES OF THE ⫸⫸⫸
AMERICAN REVOLUTION

By Robert M. Hamilton

KidHaven
PUBLISHING

Published in 2017 by
KidHaven Publishing, an Imprint of Greenhaven Publishing, LLC
353 3rd Avenue
Suite 255
New York, NY 10010

Designer: Seth Hughes
Editor: Jennifer Lombardo

Photo credits: Cover (bottom) Universal History Archive/Getty Images; Cover (top) margouillat photo/Shutterstock.com; back cover, pp. 2, 3, 9, 13, 17, 21–24 (wood texture) Maya Kruchankova/Shutterstock.com; p. 5 (Boston Tea Party illustration) Courtesy of Library of Congress; p. 6 (George Washington) Georgios Kollidas/Shutterstock.com; p. 7 littleny/Shutterstock.com; pp. 9, 13, 17, 21 (notebook) BrAt82/Shutterstock.com; p. 9 (inset) Dixie D. Vereen/For The Washington Post via Getty Images; pp. 10 (apple cider), 21 (baked beans) Brent Hofacker/Shutterstock.com; p. 11 (coffeepot) DeAgostini/Getty Images; p. 13 (raisins) amornchaijj/Shutterstock.com; p. 13 (spinach) BW Folsom/Shutterstock.com; p.14 (dried fruit) Yulla Furman/Shutterstock.com; p. 15 (honey) Artem Shadrin/Shutterstock.com; p. 16 (statue) Joseph Sohm/Shutterstock.com; p. 17 (stew) © istockphoto.com/Lisovskaya; p. 18 (coffee beans) Alexander Mazurkevich/Shutterstock.com; p. 19 (painting of woman) Bettmann/Getty Images.

Cataloging-in-Publication Data

Names: Hamilton, Robert M.
Title: Recipes of the American Revolution / Robert M. Hamilton.
Description: New York : KidHaven Publishing, 2017. | Series: Cooking your way through American history| Includes index.
Identifiers: ISBN 9781534521049 (pbk.) | ISBN 9781534521063 (library bound) | ISBN 9781534521056 (6 pack) | ISBN 9781534521070 (ebook)
Subjects: LCSH: Cooking, American–History–Juvenile literature. | United States–History–Revolution, 1775-1783–Juvenile literature.
Classification: LCC TX715.H36 2017 | DDC 641.5974'09'033–dc23

Printed in the United States of America

CPSIA compliance information: Batch #CW17KL: For further information contact Greenhaven Publishing LLC, New York, New York at 1-844-317-7404.

Please visit our website, www.greenhavenpublishing.com. For a free color catalog of all our high-quality books, call toll free 1-844-317-7404 or fax 1-844-317-7405.

CONTENTS

THE AMERICAN REVOLUTION

Before 1776, our country wasn't called the United States; instead, it was called the United Colonies. The colonies belonged to England, and England made the rules for the colonists. Everything the colonists wanted to buy from or sell to other countries had to go through England first. That way, England made money on whatever the colonists bought or sold.

By 1775, the colonists had decided they wanted to rule themselves. They wanted to be able to buy and sell their own food and goods. They also didn't like the fact that they paid taxes to England but didn't get to vote on the laws. Because England wouldn't listen to them, the colonists got angry and decided they wanted to rule their own country. This was the start of the American **Revolution**.

The colonists wanted to show England they were angry when England put a tax on tea, so they dumped boxes of tea into Boston Harbor. They called this the Boston Tea Party, and it was a big part of why the war started.

WHAT DID THE COLONISTS EAT?

In colonial America, people got their food from farming, hunting, and fishing. John was nine years old when the war began. His family lived in the city of Philadelphia, so they could go to a general store to buy things such as coffee, flour, and sugar. They also had a small garden for fruits and vegetables, chickens for eggs, and a goat for milk. Important members of government, such as George Washington and Thomas Jefferson, had large farms. They bought slaves to work on the farms for them.

Nearly everyone ate well when the crops grew well. Visitors to the colonies were amazed to see so many different kinds of food and so much of it. During the war, however, there was less food for everyone.

George Washington

Thomas Jefferson had several gardens such as this at his home in Virginia.

TRADITIONAL MEALS

Meals were different during the American Revolution than they are today. Farmers would wake up early and eat a quick breakfast that might include oatmeal or cornmeal mush with bread. John and his family ate a dish called scrapple for breakfast. It was made from cornmeal, bits of pork, and spices. Wealthy plantation owners in the South would eat breakfast later in the day and their breakfasts might include fruit pies, bread, and cold meat.

Lunch was called dinner, and it was the biggest meal of the day. People ate different foods depending on what part of the country they lived in, but a **traditional** meal might include cheese, eggs, fish, pork, stew, and vegetables. The third meal of the day was called supper, and like breakfast, it was generally a small meal that was eaten late in the evening. Often, people just ate the leftovers from breakfast and dinner.

Frumenty

Ingredients:

1 cup bulgur wheat
1 cup boiling water
¼ teaspoon salt
½ cup milk
½ cup half-and-half
½ teaspoon cinnamon
⅛ teaspoon ground mace
2 tablespoons brown sugar

Directions:

- Put the bulgur wheat and salt in a small bowl.
- Pour in the boiling water and stir. Cover and let sit for 15 minutes.
- In a medium-size pot, heat the milk and half-and-half on medium heat.
- Add the cinnamon, mace, and brown sugar.
- Stir; don't let the mixture boil.
- When the mixture is hot, add the soaked bulgur wheat and stir well.
- Cook and stir this porridge for 10 minutes. Serve.

This serves three people.

Frumenty is a northern breakfast food made from bulgur wheat, which can be found today in health food stores and some supermarkets.

WHAT DID THE COLONISTS DRINK?

The most common drinks in the colonies were cider, whiskey, coffee, and hot chocolate. Tea was popular until England taxed it, when colonists started to **boycott** it. People in the country could drink water from streams or wells, and they would send it to the cities in barrels. The water in Philadelphia and most other cities was polluted with garbage, so it wasn't safe to drink. John's mother gave him a little bit of beer or cider to drink because it wouldn't make him sick the way the water would.

John's family had a goat that gave milk, but this milk was generally used for cooking, not for drinking. It couldn't be stored for a long time because there were no refrigerators to keep it cold, so it spoiled quickly.

apple cider

Many colonists drank coffee and served it in coffeepots similar to this one.

AN UNHEALTHY DIET

Even though there was a lot of food for people to eat, they didn't know much at this time about **nutrition**, so they ate many things that made them unhealthy. They ate meat with a lot of fat on it. They often ate cream and butter, which have a lot of fat in them, too. Nobody ate raw vegetables; they were usually boiled for so long that they lost all their **vitamins**. Even salads were boiled. Fruit was usually cooked into pies or made into jam.

Many people became sick because they didn't eat nutritious foods or cook foods in ways that were good for them. Today, we eat many of the same foods the colonists ate, but we have learned how to cook them so they're nutritious. Doctors also know more about nutrition now than they did in colonial times, so they can advise their patients about which foods to eat and which to avoid.

Revolutionary Boiled Salad

Ingredients:

1 10-oz package frozen chopped
 spinach, defrosted
¼ cup raisins
2 tablespoons butter
2 tablespoons white vinegar
1 ½ teaspoons brown sugar
½ teaspoon salt

Directions:

- Drain the spinach in a
  colander, and put it in a
  medium-size pot.
- Cover the pot, put it on the
  stove, and turn the heat to medium.
- Cook the spinach for five minutes,
  stirring it a few times.
- Uncover the pot. With a large spoon,
  stir in the raisins, butter, vinegar, brown
  sugar, and salt.
- Keep cooking for five more minutes, stirring from time to time.
- Serve as a vegetable dish, not as a salad.

This serves two people.

The American colonists boiled their salads. Today, we know that salads are healthier when they're eaten raw.

DESSERTS

The colonists had something sweet at almost every meal. This included fruit tarts, pies, puddings, and cookies. Sugar was expensive, so other things were often used. Some people raised bees for honey. In the northern colonies, people tapped maple trees for the sap, which they turned into maple syrup and maple sugar.

In areas where there were no maple trees, people made sweets with dried fruits. Meat was often served with jellies, jams, or sweet fruit sauces. Wealthy people were even able to have ice cream. John's family couldn't afford ice cream, but his mother made a treat for him by pouring hot maple syrup over ice.

dried fruits

Honey was used instead of sugar in many colonial recipes.

RATIONS FOR SOLDIERS

When the war started, many men, including John's father, **volunteered** to fight for their country. A special group of army volunteers was called **minutemen**. They received daily **rations** that included a large piece of pork or beef, flour or cornmeal, dried peas or beans, and beer or whiskey. They had to cook all the food over campfires. The men would sleep six to a tent, and those six men would take turns cooking for each other.

Sometimes there wasn't enough food to go around, so the soldiers went hungry. This happened especially in the winter, when the crops couldn't grow and it was hard to **transport** food in the snow and ice.

minuteman statue

Minuteman's Beef Stew

Ingredients:
1 ½ pounds beef chuck roast
2 tablespoons vegetable oil
1 14.5-oz or 16-oz can beef broth
½ teaspoon salt
½ teaspoon ground black pepper
1 bay leaf
1 medium onion
1 clove garlic
1 medium potato
2 carrots

Directions:
- Cut the meat into bite-size pieces.
- Heat the oil in a large, heavy pot on medium-high heat. Gently add the pieces of meat.
- Stir with a large spoon until the meat is brown all over. This will take about 10 minutes.
- Pour the beef broth over the meat, and lower the heat under the pot. Add salt, pepper, and the bay leaf.
- Wait until the broth starts to boil. Stir, then cover the pot and simmer on low heat for one hour.
  - While the beef is cooking, peel and chop the onion into small pieces.
  - Peel and mince the garlic. Peel the potato and carrots, and cut them into bite-size pieces.
  - After the beef has simmered for one hour, add the onion, garlic, potatoes, and carrots. Bring stew to a boil over low heat.
  - Cover the pot and simmer for 30 more minutes.
- Serve stew with bread and butter.

This serves four to five people.

Minutemen cooked their food over campfires, which took longer than cooking on a stove. Remember to always ask for an adult's help when cooking.

RIOTS OVER FOOD SHORTAGES

The women who stayed at home during the war, such as John's mother, faced food shortages because most of the food was sent to the army. Merchants in the cities who sold food items such as coffee, sugar, and flour would sometimes charge very high prices because they knew people were desperate enough to pay almost anything. This made the women very angry, and in some places they led **riots**.

In one riot in Boston, a group of women told one merchant that he needed to charge less for coffee and sugar. When he wouldn't agree, they took the keys to his warehouse and stole the coffee!

sack of coffee

Women rioted during the American Revolution because greedy merchants were overcharging for items such as sugar and coffee.

THE END OF THE WAR

The American Revolution ended in 1783, when John was 17 years old. England lost, so it no longer controlled the United States. However, starting a new country was hard work. The war was expensive, so there wasn't a lot of extra money or food to go around for a few years. John's family had to eat simple meals, and sometimes they couldn't get food they were used to eating.

Over time, the **economy** of the United States got better, so people had more money. People from other countries started coming to the United States to live, and they brought foods and recipes from their old countries. Because of this, Americans today have more types of foods to choose from than the colonists did.

Boston Baked Beans

Ingredients:
6 cups canned navy beans
1 medium onion
1 tablespoon dry mustard powder
1 teaspoon ground black pepper
1 ½ teaspoons salt
1 ½ tablespoons white vinegar
¼ cup molasses
1 piece smoked pork shoulder, neck, or ham bone

Directions:
- Preheat the oven to 250° Fahrenheit (F).
- Chop the onion into small pieces.
- Mix all the ingredients together in a large, heavy baking pan with a lid.
- Add enough water to cover the beans. Stir again. Make sure the meat is under the liquid.
- Put the lid on the pan, and put the pan in the oven.
- Bake for five hours. Stir beans at least twice during baking. If the beans seem dry, add a little water.
- Thirty minutes before beans are finished baking, take off the lid. Continue to bake uncovered.
- When finished, take the pot out of the oven, and serve the beans with cornbread.

This serves six people.

This dish is still popular today, but the recipe has changed over time. This recipe is the way the colonists used to make it.

GLOSSARY

boycott: To refuse to buy, use, or participate in something as a way of protesting.

economy: The amount of buying and selling in a place.

minutemen: People who volunteered to fight in the American Revolution and could be "ready to march in a minute."

nutrition: Anything that a living thing needs for energy, to grow, or to heal.

rations: A fixed amount of food given to a person.

revolution: A complete change in government.

riots: Situations in which a large group of people behaves in a violent and uncontrolled way.

traditional: Having to do with the ways of doing things in a culture that are passed down from parents to children.

transport: To move someone or something from one place to another.

vitamins: Nutrients that help the body fight illness and grow strong.

volunteer: To do something to help because you want to do it.

FOR MORE INFORMATION

WEBSITES

Chronicle of the Revolution
www.pbs.org/ktca/liberty/chronicle.html
Read fun "news articles" about important events in the American Revolution.

Colonial America: Food and Cooking
www.ducksters.com/history/colonial_america/food.php
Learn more about what the colonists ate and their mealtime customs.

Colonial Foodways
www.history.org/Foundation/journal/Autumn04/food.cfm
This article gives more information about the differences between the way the wealthy and the poor ate. The "Kids" tab on the site has games and activities.

BOOKS

Cabral, Patrick. *Black Patriots in the American Revolutionary War: The Untold Story.* Topeka, KS: Embracing Legacy, LLC, 2015.

Marciniak, Kristin. *The Revolutionary War: Why They Fought.* North Mankato, MN: Compass Point Books, 2016.

Raum, Elizabeth. *At Battle in the Revolutionary War: An Interactive Battlefield Adventure.* North Mankato, MN: Capstone Press, 2015.

INDEX